From the Flyers Minor Atom A Team

Thanks to My Hockey Coach

To All Hockey Coaches with Respect and Thanks

Toronto, Ontario, Canada

Copyright 2010 © Jason Howell

All rights reserved. No part of this work covered by the copyrights hereon may be reproduced or used in any form or by any means—graphic, electronic or mechanical, including photocopying, recording, taping or information storage and retrieval systems—without the prior written permission of the publisher, or, in case of photocopying or other reprographic copying, a licence from Access Copyright, the Canadian Copyright Licensing Agency, One Yonge Street, Suite 1900, Toronto, Ontario, M6B 3A9.

The publisher gratefully acknowledges the support of the Canada Council for the Arts and the Ontario Arts Council for its publishing program. We acknowledge the support of the Government of Ontario through the Ontario Media Development Corporation's Ontario Book Initiative.

We acknowledge the financial support of the Government of Canada through the Canada Book Fund (CBF) for our publishing activities.

KPk is an imprint of
Key Porter Books Limited
Six Adelaide Street East, Tenth Floor
Toronto, Ontario, Canada M5C 1H6

www.keyporter.com

Printed and bound in Canada
10 11 12 13 14 5 4 3 2 1

Library and Archives Canada Cataloguing in Publication

Thanks to My Hockey Coach / Flyers Minor Atom A Team.

ISBN 978-155470-392-0

1. Hockey players--Ontario--Orangeville.
2. Coaches and players. I. Flyers Minor Atom A Team (Hockey Team)

GV848.5.A1I3 2009   796.962092'271341   C2009-904721-7

this book is dedicated to all
hockey coaches
with respect and thanks

contributors Ben F, Ben S, Cade B, Cameron L, Cameron M, Carter T, Conner H, Dawson C, Ethan D, Ethan S, Harrison M, Jacob S, Liam M, Myles H, Travis B, Trevor A

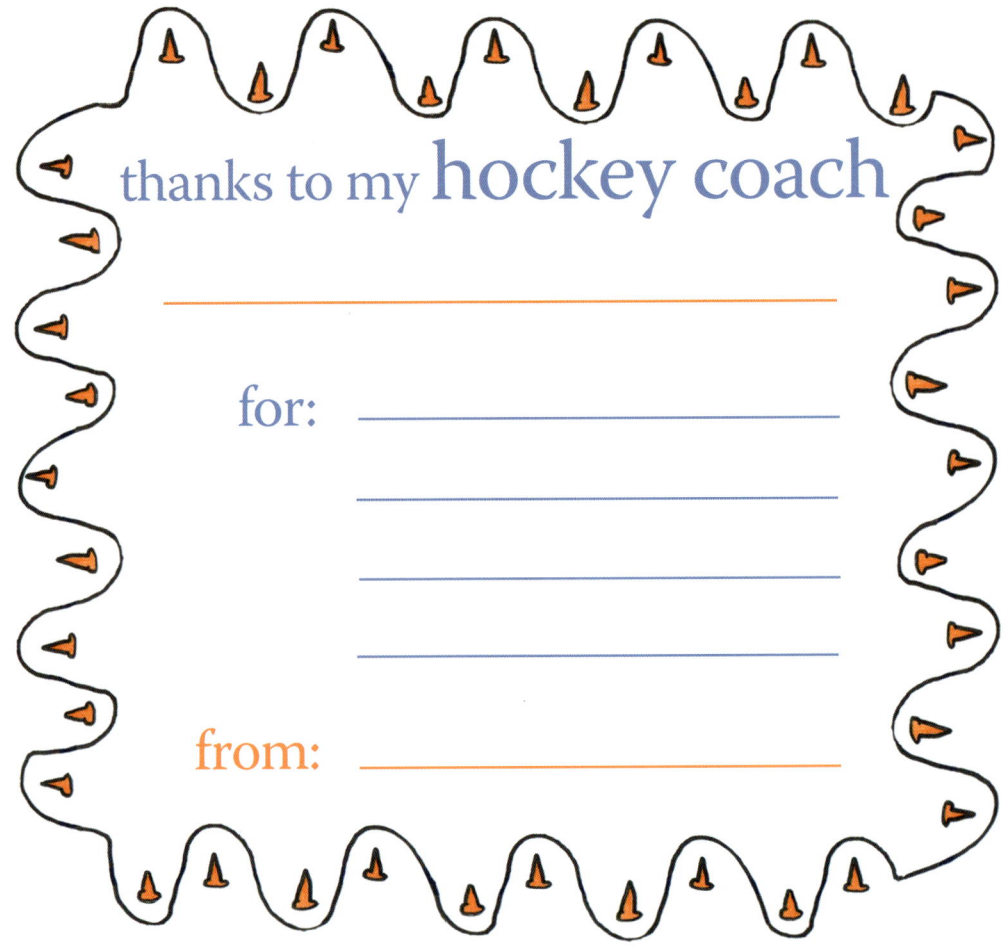

and here is my drawing for you, Coach!

introduction

The first time you volunteered to coach hockey, I am guessing you didn't think about it too much in advance. You probably didn't add up all the hours you would need to commit to planning practices, organizing tournaments, and developing game strategies. Oh, and you probably didn't fully understand that dealing with the kids is one thing…but dealing with the parents is another (the kids are the easy part, let's be honest 😊).

Instead, you went with your heart, because you felt you had something to contribute…and we're glad you did, because you have contributed. You have made a big difference in the education and mentoring of a group of kids, a group who will forever call you "Coach."

When our then-Novice AE rep team set out last year to honour hockey moms and hockey dads, with the books *I Love My Hockey Mom* and *Thanks to My Hockey Dad*, it became clear from the very beginning that the story would be incomplete without thanking you, the hockey coach. So the kids went back to do more "hockey homework," under the direction of teacher Jennifer Sutoski, and this new project, *Thanks to My Hockey Coach*, was born.

The players put together this charming and funny tribute to all hockey coaches. Drawing on their experiences, past and present, they thank their coaches less for wins on the scoreboard and more for the funny and silly memories, the teaching time, and the skill-building. The bond between coaches and players can be a strong one, a lifelong one, and on behalf of all the kids you have coached, we want to thank you for displaying those qualities that are the best in all of us—patience, heart, fairness—all while walking that tightrope of "just having fun."

Sometimes all a player needs is a kick in the goal pads before a game—a kick that says "I believe in you" or "I want you to succeed." We sometimes forget that coaches need that confidence and support, too. Coach, we believed in you, too, and you succeeded.

Thanks for everything!

jason howell Flyers Minor Atom A coach

thanks to my
hockey coach
for making me a better

stickhandler

and skater

and for not getting
mad at me when
i take a penalty.

thanks to my
hockey coach
for organizing
a post-game

snack list

and for
cheering me up
when i was on the

disabLed

list.

ben s.

thanks to my hockey coach for teaching me to use **one hand on the stick** to skate faster, and to always pump my arms when i am skating and for *squirting water* in my m⊚uth when i come in off a shift.

thanks to my hockey coach for playing the music

really loud

because it gets us **pumped up** and ready to play

and
for all the fun
at our hockey tournaments, like throwing us in the *pool.*

thanks to my hockey coach for giving up your time and not even getting paid

and for sometimes
yelling
at the refs.

thanks to my hockey coach for explaining drills twice if i do not understand

and thanks to
my dad,
who helped coach me
when i was little.
We had a rink in our
backyard, and he
showed me how to
skate and shoot.

thanks to my hockey coach for telling me to get up off the ice after i'm *hit*—unless i am bleeding, dying, or broken,

conner h.

but then if i don't get up, he comes over to me and says "nice job for taking that *hit*."

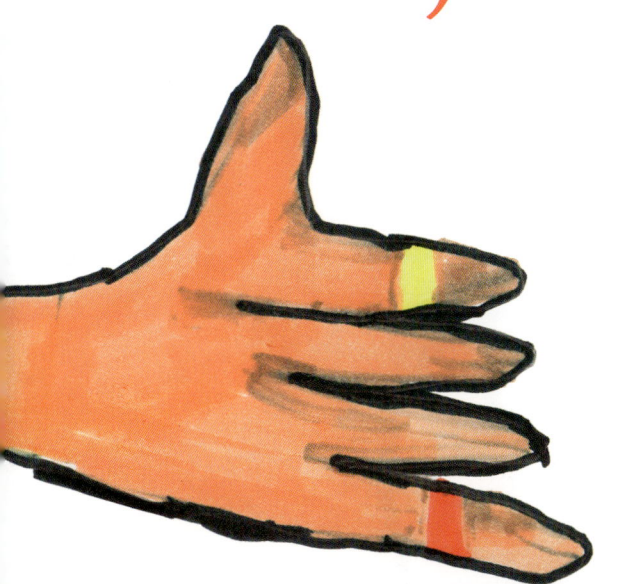

conner h.

thanks to my hockey coach for teaching me that it's just as important to **stop** goals as it is to **get** goals and for teaching me

to

never

give

up ♥

thanks to my hockey coach for wearing a wig one time at a game that got my attention and for putting little mascots on the bench every game...the people in the seats really like them.

carter t.

thanks to my hockey coach for keeping the game safe by pointing out when the refs miss a penalty

and for making sure that
i always leave with a
smile on my face,
no matter what happens
on the ice.

carter t.

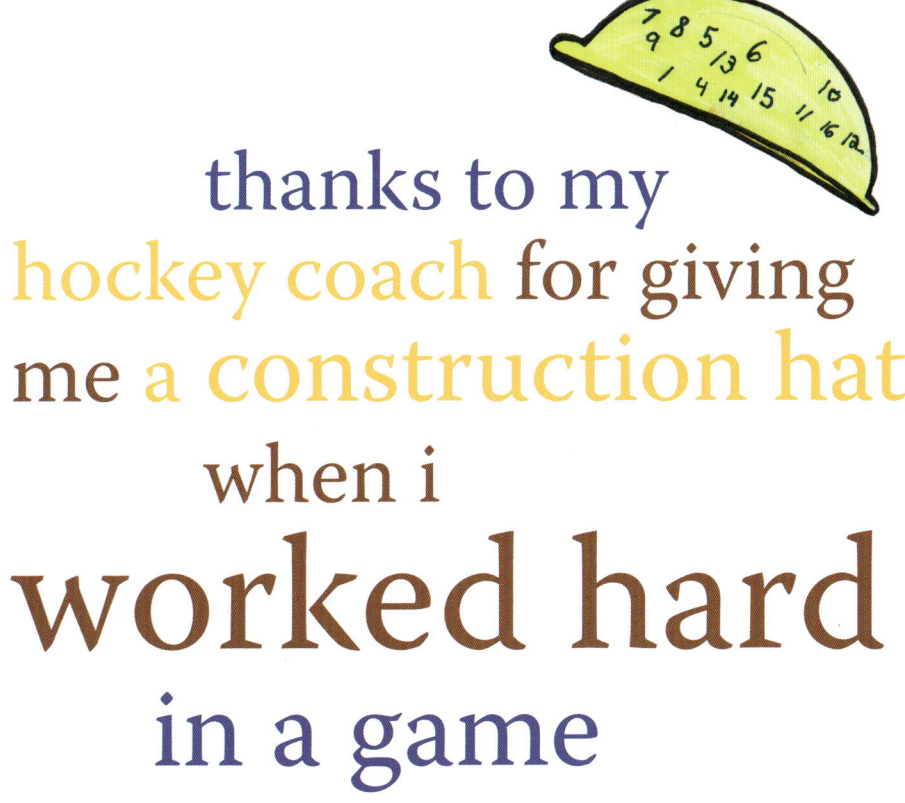

thanks to my hockey coach for giving me a construction hat when i worked hard in a game and for **brightening up** my day with man-to-man talks.

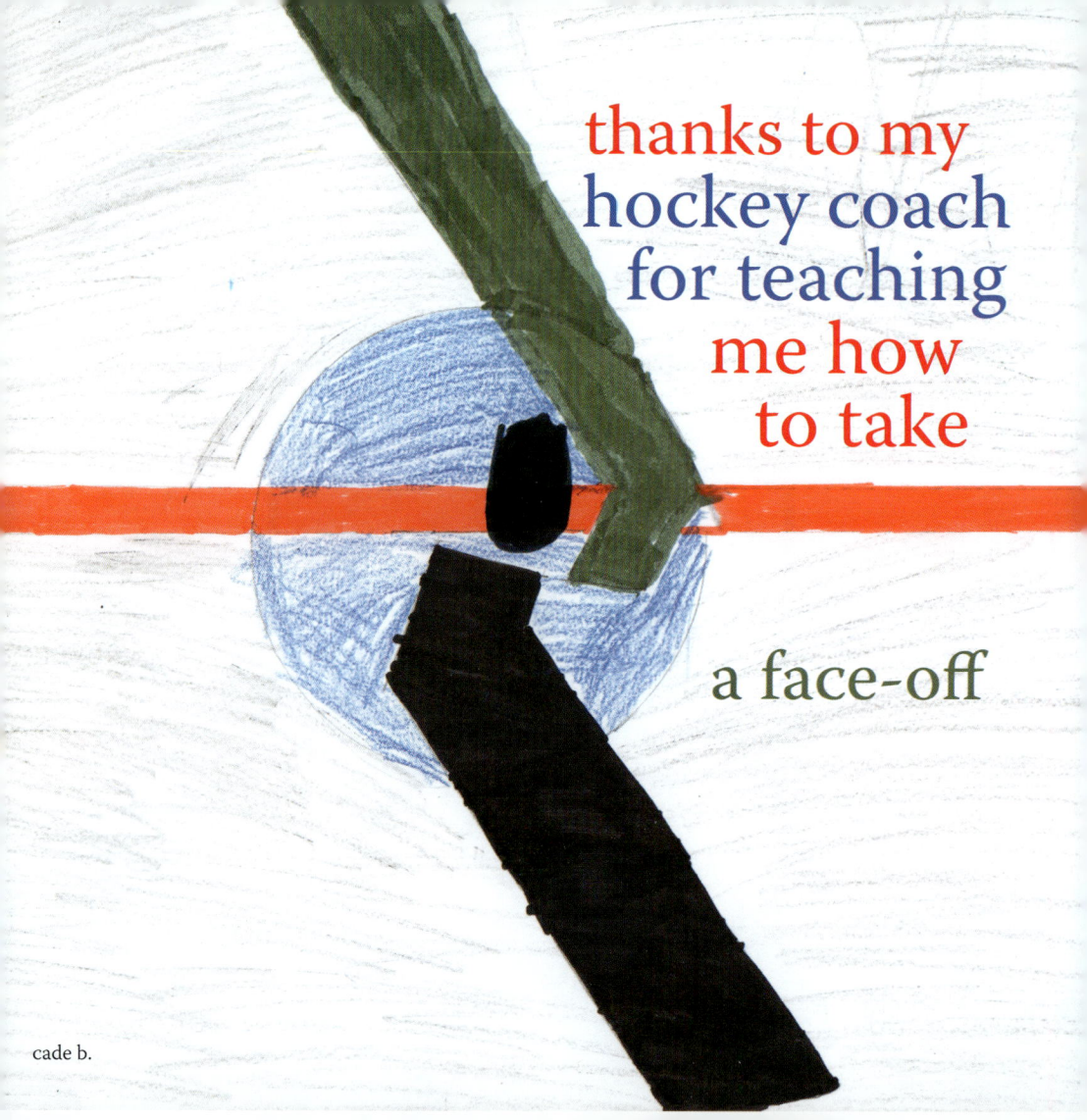

and for making practices

fun.

cade b.

myles h.

thanks to my hockey coach for helping me with

my moves.

and for letting us drink strawberry stuff out of our trophies.

thanks to my hockey coach for putting me on the same line as my friends and thanks for sticking up for me, when i got *elbowed* in the face.

thanks to my
hockey coach
for believing in
us

and for having such

fun team parties.

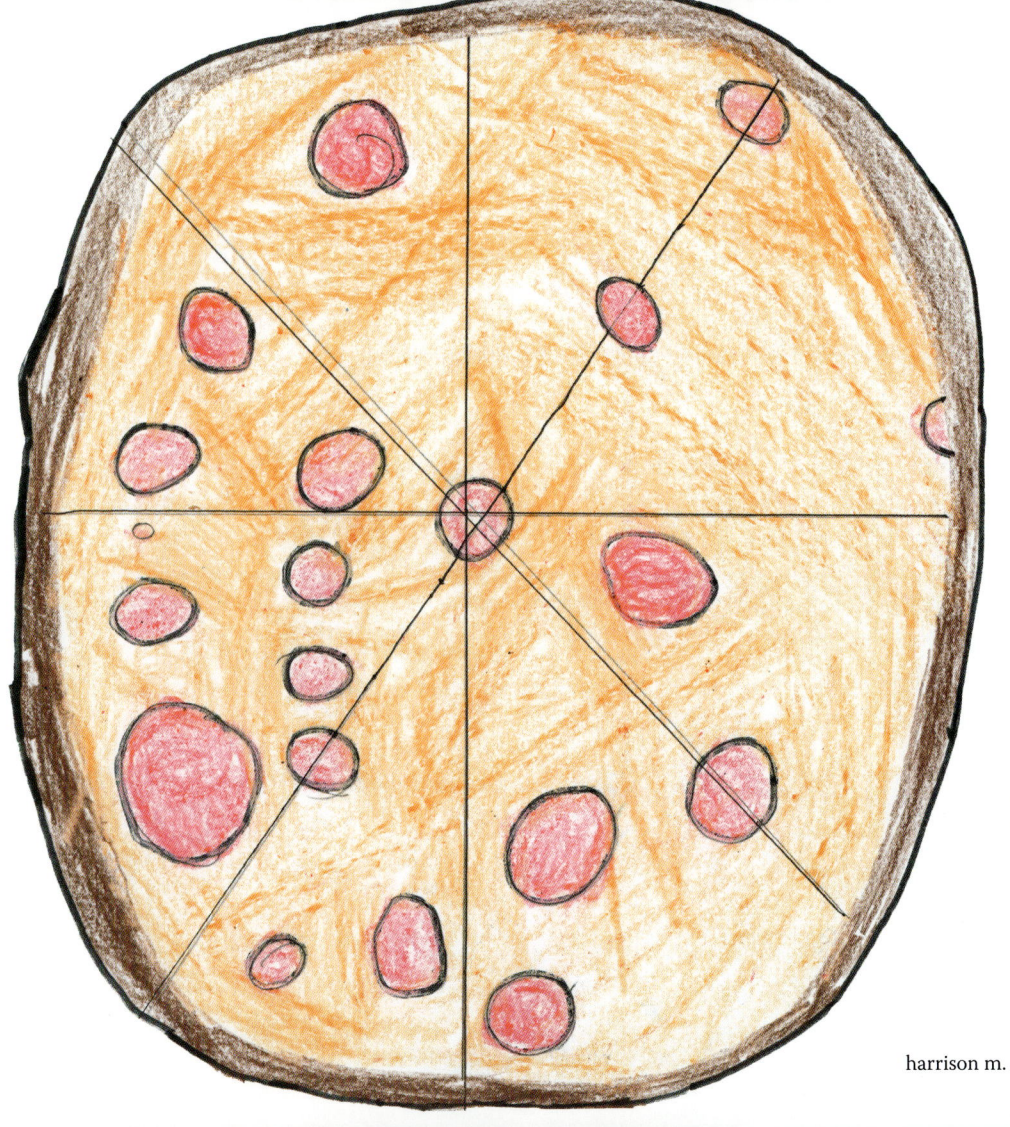

harrison m.

thanks to my
hockey coach for

picking me up

when i needed

a ride

and for teaching us that teammates *pass* the **puck** to each other — we got it!

cameron m.